EXPLORING THE WORLD OF
Alligators and Crocodiles

Tracy C. Read

FIREFLY BOOKS

A Firefly Book

Published by Firefly Books Ltd. 2017

First printing

Publisher Cataloging-in-Publication Data (U.S.)
Names: Read, Tracy C., author.
Title: Exploring the World of Alligators and Crocodiles / Tracy C. Read.
Description: Richmond Hill, Ontario, Canada : Firefly Books, 2017. | Series: Exploring the world of --- | Includes index. | Summary: "Up-close images and fascinating facts about alligators and crocodiles" – Provided by publisher.
Identifiers: ISBN 978-1-77085-942-5 (hardcover) | 978-1-77085-943-2 (paperback)
Subjects: LCSH: Alligators – Juvenile literature. | Crocodiles – Juvenile literature.
Classification: LCC QL666.C925R433 | DDC 597.98 – dc23

Library and Archives Canada Cataloguing in Publication
Read, Tracy C., author
        Exploring the world of alligators and crocodiles / Tracy C. Read.
Includes index.
ISBN 978-1-77085-942-5 (hardcover).--ISBN 978-1-77085-943-2 (softcover)
        1. Alligators--Juvenile literature. 2. Crocodiles--Juvenile literature.
I. Title.
QL666.C925R43 2017   j597.98   C2017-902459-0

Published in the United States by
Firefly Books (U.S.) Inc.
P.O. Box 1338, Ellicott Station, Buffalo, New York 14205

Published in Canada by
Firefly Books Ltd.
50 Staples Avenue, Unit 1, Richmond Hill, Ontario L4B 0A7

Cover and interior design: Janice McLean/Bookmakers Press Inc.

Printed in China

We acknowledge the financial support of the Government of Canada.

For Dean, defender of dragons.

Front cover: © Whirler/iStock

Back cover: © Ondrej Prosicky/Shutterstock

Back cover, inset, left:
    © WeStudio/Shutterstock

Back cover, inset, right top:
    © Jolanda Aalbers/Shutterstock

Back cover, inset, right bottom:
    © John Swanepoel/Shutterstock

CONTENTS

NOSE TIPS

The U-shaped snouts of these young crocodilians instantly identify them as American alligators. As they socialize on a sun-splashed log, a protective mother is almost certainly close by.

MEET THE CROCODILIANS

Some 230 million years ago, reptiles ruled the world alongside the dinosaurs and the pterosaurs, the flying reptiles. Respect is due: Only the ancestors of the crocodilians emerged from the great extinction events and the planet-transforming series of ice ages that set the stage for the mammals to take over.

Today, 24 recognized species of the Crocodylia order still live on Earth, divided into three families. The alligator family has two true members, the American and Chinese alligators, which prefer the temperate weather of the southern United States and eastern China, respectively. The other six members are known as caimans—crocodilians that live in the marshes and wetlands and along rivers and lakes in tropical Central and South America.

The crocodile family has 14 members. One of these, the American crocodile, shares some territory with the American alligator as well as a handful of other crocodiles and caimans in the New World. The rest are found in tropical and subtropical regions in Africa, Asia and Australia.

The two species in the gharial family, the gharial and tomistoma, formerly the false gharial, are native to South Asia.

With armored skin and a snoutful of gnarly teeth, these creatures—the most advanced of all the reptiles—inspire fear and respect in humans. Let's find out how these cold-blooded cousins of the dinosaurs beat the odds.

I SPY

A crocodilian's low profile in the water helps conceal its true size. A male American alligator, shown here, typically tops out at less than 13 feet (4 m) long and likes all aquatic habitats in the southern United States, from marshes and swamps to rivers and lakes.

ANATOMY LESSON

Unlike warm-blooded animals, the cold-blooded crocodilian relies on its surroundings to set its body temperature. The decision to bask in the sun or take a dip in a cool river is all about internal climate control.

Symmetrical and streamlined, the low-built crocodilian has a burly swimmer's physique. Floating with its head on the surface, it uses its rear legs for stability as its body rests at an almost vertical angle in the water. Only its back feet are webbed, to accommodate swift launches and turns. It deploys its muscular tail for propulsion, reaching speeds of 20 miles per hour (32 km/h).

On land, the croc uses its short limbs in a range of awkward gaits, from a belly crawl and a "high walk" to an occasional gallop, at speeds of up to 10 miles per hour (16 km/h).

Every crocodilian is clad head to toe in bony, durable scales that protect it from internal injuries during battles with other crocs. Its prey stand little chance against the deadly power of its jaws.

This reptile's internal organs have also evolved for the crocodilian lifestyle. Strong stomach enzymes quickly digest flesh and bone, and a uniquely structured four-chambered heart allows blood to be mixed outside the ventricles, an advantage for a diving reptile that is able to hold its breath underwater for up to an hour when submerged.

CROC SMILES

A crocodilian's upper and lower teeth intermesh when its jaws are closed, as shown in the endangered Chinese alligator, top. The yacare caiman, middle, bares its sharp, conical teeth, while the slender-snouted gharial, above, looks as if its jaws are zippered shut.

WARMED FOR BATTLE

The cold-blooded crocodilian counts on the warmth of the sun to keep its muscles in working order. Note the raised scales on this American alligator's back. Well supplied with blood vessels, these osteoderms collect and transport heat into the body while the crocodilian basks in the sun. With no sweat glands, it cools its brain by "mouth gaping," not unlike a panting dog.

The American and Chinese alligators have a short, broad, U-shaped snout, while that of most crocodiles and caimans is longer, narrower and V-shaped. The fish-eating gharials set a new standard with an elongated, slender jaw crammed with 110 teeth.

Tail power
Long trunk muscles extend into the crocodilian's tail, which is the prime source of propulsion when it is swimming.

Scales
The crocodilian's skin is covered with rows of squarish, tightly placed horny scales that serve as protection.

Limbs
The short legs of the crocodilian are straddled sideways from its body, rather than positioned directly underneath it.

Temperature tweaking
The ideal internal temperature of a crocodilian is between 86 and 91.5 degrees F (30°–33°C). It self-regulates by lying in the sun or shade, dipping into a cool river or mouth gaping.

Webbed feet
A crocodilian uses its webbed rear feet to launch itself from a resting position, rather than to paddle.

Tick-tock
Small undigestible items can stay in a crocodilian's stomach for a long time, and researchers exploit this by feeding crocs radio transmitters used to track them.

Head
Regardless of species, a crocodilian's flat head is typically one-seventh of its total body length and is designed for "minimum exposure" in the water.

Fully loaded
Large close-set eyes sit atop the crocodilian's head, with the ears placed closely behind. Sight, hearing and smell are all in play when the croc's head is above water.

Tongue
Most crocodiles have salt glands on the underside of their fleshy tongue. These glands are used to excrete excess salt when the crocs venture into ocean water.

Teeth
Crocodilian teeth are designed to pierce and hold, rather than cut and chew. Each time a tooth falls out, another erupts under it. Teeth are replaced roughly every 20 months, though that pace slows as the croc ages.

Jaws of death
When biting down on its prey, the Nile crocodile can exert as much as 5,000 pounds of pressure per square inch. Humans apply 100 pounds per square inch.

Length
The second largest crocodilian (after the saltwater croc), the Nile crocodile, shown here, can grow to lengths greater than 17 feet (5 m).

NATURAL TALENTS

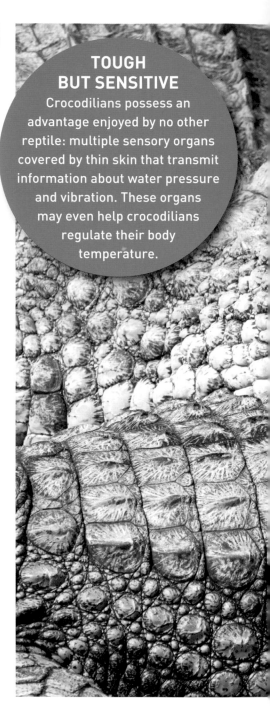

TOUGH BUT SENSITIVE
Crocodilians possess an advantage enjoyed by no other reptile: multiple sensory organs covered by thin skin that transmit information about water pressure and vibration. These organs may even help crocodilians regulate their body temperature.

The element of surprise is the most important tool in this semiaquatic carnivore's tool kit, and all five senses are specially designed to play a role.

Crocodilans unleash a lightning-quick attack on their prey when an opportunity appears. As they lurk, motionless, with their eyes, ears and nostrils just above water, these efficient hunters are able to take advantage of sound, sight and smell simultaneously.

This reptile does most of its work at dusk or night. Its large, close-set eyes, positioned prominently on top of its head, feature the vertical pupils common to nocturnal hunters, such as owls, geckos, vipers and cats. The pupils defensively narrow to slits in the bright light of day but open wide at dark, letting in all the available light. In addition, as with other night-hunting animals, the crocodilian's eyeballs feature a layer of tissue called the tapetum lucidum, which improves sight by reflecting light back into the retina. Transparent eyelids slide across the eyes for protection when a crocodilian is underwater or attacking prey.

The reptile's narrow ear openings are located just behind its eyes and are protected by a skin flap that prevents water from entering its ears during a dive. Above water, its hearing is considered better than average compared with other reptiles, and it is highly sensitive to a wide range of sounds. The crocodilian is extremely communicative—the male lets loose

THE DETECTORISTS

Above: Noses in the air, these crocodilians relax as they sniff out their surroundings. Below: The crocodilian's hallmark vertical pupil. With its prominent, close-set eyes, a crocodilian enjoys binocular vision and typically faces its prey before attacking. In defense, it can pull its eyeballs into its eye sockets.

with loud courtship bellows, a nest-guarding female issues hissing calls to discourage egg-snatchers, and a juvenile is always eager to share its distress vocally.

With nostrils that lead to scent-detecting chambers and a brain that features large olfactory lobes, the crocodilian has a well-developed sense of smell. As with other body openings, the nostrils are equipped with a protective flap. The crocodilian also has taste buds, though not a lot is known about this sense.

Perhaps the most intriguing crocodilian sense is touch. The heavily armored crocodilian has built-in ultrasensitive touch sensors that detect changes in water pressure and vibration. In alligators, these are scattered around the jaw; in crocodiles, they are distributed all over the body. This adaptation may help the crocodilian establish a prey's precise location before attacking. On a gentler note, it may also account for the crocodilian's ability to delicately carry its hatchlings in its lethal jaws without harming them.

HEARING
Crocodilians have excellent hearing and can pick up a wide range of sounds.

SIGHT
Nocturnal hunters, the crocodilians have vertical pupils that shut out daylight but open wide to let in available light at night.

SMELL
With large olfactory lobes that manage scent, crocodilians are well equipped to sniff out prey and family members.

TOUCH
Alligators and crocodiles are sensitive to touch. Mating animals use their mouths and bodies to express interest.

TASTE
Like all carnivores, crocodilians have a wide-ranging appetite for fresh meat.

TOUCH[2]
The tiny black dots located around this young alligator's jaws are sensory organs that can detect even slight changes in water pressure.

IT'S COMPLICATED

Don't be fooled by their ferocious appearance—crocodilians are very interested in the language of love.

While male and female crocodilians don't form lasting relationships—dominant male crocodilians mate with several females during the breeding season—they do engage in a variety of complex courtship behaviors.

Inspired by warm, humid weather, a male Nile crocodile in Africa travels several miles to a nesting beach, where he chases off his competition by bursting out of the water, his neck swelled and his teeth bared. To express his romantic interest, a male caiman in South America raises his head and lifts his tail vertically out of the water. A male mugger crocodile in the Indian subcontinent cruises his territory with his back and tail on display, reinforcing his superiority with intimidating "headslaps" that resound across the water.

The female crocodilian is not a passive bystander in the mating ritual. To express her interest, a female mugger swims past a male with her head raised. A female American alligator nudges and bumps against the head and neck of her chosen mate. In India, a female gharial lifts her long snout skyward to signal her readiness.

Mating always takes place underwater and, depending on the species, can be over in 30 seconds or last up to 30 minutes.

Some three to six weeks later,

THE DATING GAME

Before mating, male and female crocodilians indulge in a wide variety of courtship behaviors, from raising their tails and heads out of the water to an extensive round of nudging and snout rubbing. Some take turns pushing one another underwater, perhaps to measure strength. Although crocodilians always mate below the surface, the much larger male Nile crocodile seen here is making his intentions clear on land.

before laying her eggs, the female prepares a nest. Alligators and caimans gather fresh vegetation, leaf litter and soil to make mound nests for their eggs, as do several crocodile species. Others, including the gharial and the mugger, Australian freshwater, Nile and Orinoco crocodiles, favor a hole dug into a sand-bar or the shore of a river or lake. Once the eggs are laid—between 20 and 80, depending on the species—the mother carefully covers them to conceal the nest from predators and to incubate the eggs at the right temperature. The father sometimes helps out with this task and occasionally guards the nest as well. Incubation lasts some 35 days with smaller crocodilian species and 90 to 100 days for larger species. Throughout, the mother stays close at hand until the hatchlings chip their way out of the eggs. Then she may gently pick up each one in her muscular jaws and carry them to water.

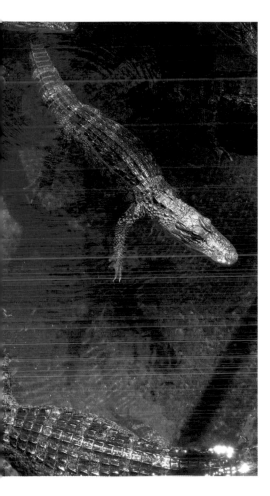

Crocodilian young face perils both as unhatched eggs and as hatchlings. Flooding and sudden drops in temperature may end the embryo's life before it hatches. Raccoons, skunks, bears and otters all raid the nests of the American alligators, while the eggs of caimans and crocodiles in South America are scooped up by coatis, lizards and monkeys. Monitor lizards throughout the ranges of many species are also a major threat. And the predators of hatchlings are too many to mention, from birds and bears to turtles and snakes. For the young crocodilian, the world is a dangerous place. Payback comes later.

WE ARE FAMILY

An American alligator juvenile catches a ride with Mom, above. Generations of youngsters may enjoy the protection of their female parent and later form their own loose-knit social groups. While sticking close to mother reduces risk, gathering in large, mixed-age groups is also a fairly common crocodilian behavior.

COLD-BLOODED TERMINATORS

TROUBLE IN MIND
A Nile crocodile pulls itself onshore in Kruger National Park, South Africa. If this crocodile has had a recent meal, it might simply be looking for a place to lie in the sun. Otherwise, these shorebirds had better stay alert.

Encased in scaly armor, with a bony head meant to crack skulls, a mouth full of sharp, menacing teeth that can puncture and grip and a powerful, streamlined tail designed to pack a wallop, crocodilians are natural-born killers.

Crocodilians eat almost anything, even fruit, though their primary interest is in other living creatures. What's for dinner can depend on where they live and the season. As a general rule, the broader-snouted species, like the black caiman, the mugger and the Nile crocodiles, seek out more robust prey, while the slender-snouted crocodilians, such as the gharial and the Australian and New Guinea freshwater crocodiles, are fish-eaters. When the weather is cool, crocodilians tend to fast, but their appetites increase in the spring and summer.

Found in freshwater wetlands from North Carolina to Texas, the American alligator may venture inland on warm nights, exploring nearby trails and roadsides in hopes of encountering a night-active mammal. Adult alligator snacks might include crabs, fish, turtles, frogs, snakes, birds and small mammals, like muskrat, otter and possum. A hatchling gets by on lighter fare—insects, snails and worms and perhaps a passing butterfly, if the budding predator is quick enough to leap up and snatch it.

But whether it's an American alligator lurking in the everglades or a Nile crocodile coasting silently

BOTTOMS UP

Underwater, crocodilians have a throat valve that closes to prevent water from entering the throat. They eat their prey whole when they can, but first they position it in their mouth so that it slides down smoothly. Once it reaches the croc's highly acidic stomach, this fish will be completely digested. Roughly 60 percent of the energy is stored as body fat to be used when the hunting isn't so easy.

through the reeds, dinnertime can be a dramatic, brutal attack that ends badly for prey of all descriptions. Crocodilians can't chew their food. Instead, they either swallow it whole or dismember it and eat it piece by piece.

Crocodilians often employ the classic sit-and-wait strategy, resting quietly in shallow water, eyes, ears and nostrils just breaking the surface, as they wait to see, hear and smell their unsuspecting prey. In a surge of terrifying speed, a crocodilian launches itself explosively from the water, sometimes roaring onto a beach to snap up an animal peacefully approaching the water's edge to quench its thirst. The larger crocodilians anticipate the habits of

HIDING IN PLAIN SIGHT
Camouflaged coloration and a long, streamlined body allow alligators and crocodiles to keep a low profile when in the water. But even a large crocodilian can explode from a river and leap five feet (1.5 m) into the air to snatch a bird.

their prey, appearing at well-used river crossing points or watering holes. Some linger beneath the nests of large birds, such as herons or storks, on the lookout for a careless landing too close to the water.

Nile crocodiles join forces to trap their prey. In a lake in South Africa, they have been observed gathering to take advantage of the annual migration of shoal fish.

The crocodiles cooperate by forming a line to prevent the fish from passing through, then snapping them up as they arrive.

This species also works together to dismember the carcass of a large animal, such as a tough-skinned adult buffalo or hippopotamus. Dozens patiently wait their turn, as one crocodile pins the prey and another tears off a chunk to eat.

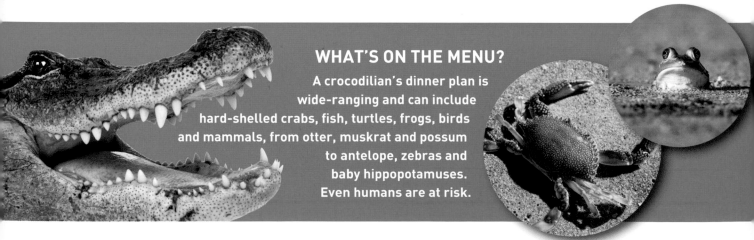

WHAT'S ON THE MENU?
A crocodilian's dinner plan is wide-ranging and can include hard-shelled crabs, fish, turtles, frogs, birds and mammals, from otter, muskrat and possum to antelope, zebras and baby hippopotamuses. Even humans are at risk.

THE WALKING DEAD

With its hind leg trapped in a crocodile's jaws, this 570-pound (260 kg) blue wildebeest in southern Africa has little chance of escape. A crocodilian's preferred strategy is to seize its prey by the nose and walk it into the water, where it is quickly drowned and devoured.

AN UNEASY TRUCE

North Americans began slaughtering vast numbers of American alligators and crocodiles to feed a post-American Civil War appetite for footwear and accessories made from crocodilian skin. Fashions come and go, and this one burst back on the scene after the Second World War. To satisfy a worldwide demand, commercial hunting of crocodiles in Africa, Southeast Asia, Australia and the Pacific Islands and of caimans in South America became so widespread in the 1950s, 1960s and 1970s that the populations of most species were threatened.

By the mid-1970s, we began to formally acknowledge the value of protecting endangered species. Many countries signed an international agreement on trade that protected crocodilians and recognized their essential role in ecosystems throughout their ranges. Crocodile farming became an accepted strategy for satisfying the demand for crocodilian skin and meat.

Wild crocodilian populations have rebounded, but humans have to be alert to the very real dangers of living among these silent, efficient predators. Wherever crocodilians are found, there is potential conflict with people, whether they are tourists in Florida, villagers washing in the river, farmers working in a lakeside field or fishermen who need to feed their families.

It's a steep but necessary price to pay to ensure that this ancient order of reptiles endures.

Saltwater Crocodile
Tropical regions of Asia and the Pacific
Up to 23 feet (7 m)

Cuvier's Dwarf Caiman (young)
Throughout central South America
Up to 5 feet (1.5 m)

Australian Freshwater Crocodile
Northern Territory, Australia
Up to 10 feet (3 m)

Siamese Crocodile
Southeast Asia
Less than 13 feet (4 m)

American Crocodile
Southern Florida, Central America,
Venezuela, Colombia
Up to 20 feet (6 m)

Black Caiman
Throughout central South America
Up to 20 feet (6 m)

Mugger Crocodile
India, Pakistan, Nepal, Sri Lanka, Iran
Over 13 feet (4 m)

American Alligator
Southeastern United States
11 to 16 feet (3.4–5 m)